Images From a Pensive Mind

By Cassie Merko

A
Pause For Poetry ©
Publication

ISBN: 978-0-9916853-8-7

Printed in Canada
January 2014

Cover Photograph: "Peace" © Gloria Swoboda

TABLE OF CONTENTS

~~~~ PHILOSOPHY ~~~~

~~~~ SPECIAL OCCASIONS ~~~~

~~~~ WHIMSY AND HUMOR ~~~~

Philosophy

A Dreamer's Dream

I ask not for fame and fortune
Or great mansions trimmed with gold
Give me but a hazel thicket
And a loving hand to hold.
A babbling brook outside my window
The soft whisper of a breeze
Grassy meadows all around me
And wild songbirds in the trees.
Give me perfume of the roses
Wafting sweetly through the air
The droning hum of bumblebees
Sipping nectar hidden there.
Give me cobwebs mid the posies
Glistening bright in the morning dew
Morning glories day proclaiming
In deep pink and azure blue.
Give me butterflies on my daisies
Soft white clouds in the sky above
Tender arms to gently hold me
In sweet bondage of true love.
Sweet solitude I'll treasure
Its serenity divine
In profusion, simple pleasure
That great "fortune" that's all mine.

Give Me Time

Let me revel in the splendour
Of a blazing sunset
Reflecting on a glassy lake
Its shimmering hues
Rivalling the heavens above.

Let me bask in the glow
Of an evening campfire
Brilliant tendrils of flickering flames
Reaching into the darkness
Like outstretched arms
Eager to embrace the night

Allow me the luxury of a leisurely walk
Ambling through lush green meadows
Musing on the shyness of the violet
Watching wild daisies bow their heads
To hoards of working bees
And eager flamboyant butterflies.

Let me savour the ticklish trek
Of a misguided bumble bee
On my outstretched arm
Searching for that nectar he'll never find.

Grant me that enchanted moment
To smell the velvety chasm
Of an orange tiger lily
Mindless of the brown smear
That stains my nose when I get too close.

Permit me to relax serenely
On a rushy shore of a meandering brook
A refreshing coolness caressing my bare toes
And a soft breeze toying with my hair.

Let me listen to the haunting cry of a distant loon
And the bark and howl of a lonely coyote
Echoing through the evening hush.

Let me forget for a moment
The must-be-done tasks
Those endless mundane chores
That always wait for me
And must be done – again

And again,

    and again,

        and again......

If Life Gave Notice

If life were to give me notice
That my journey ends tomorrow
Would I see flashes of regret?
Would I feel pangs of sorrow?

I know my dirty dishes
Would not really matter much
Nor would I feel a bit contrite
At leaving dust untouched.

I would regret not having gone
On that trip when the kids were small
And missed the rapture in their eyes
When they saw that waterfall.

I'd miss the croaking of the frogs
Of spring's overflowing creek beds
Walking, searching for new blossoms
Of marsh marigolds in the wetlands

I'd miss the gentle raindrops
Of summer's slow warm rain
'Cause my hairdo I had wished to save
How could I have been so vain?

I'd wish I'd stayed outdoors just to watch
The stars on a bright summer night
Instead of wasting precious time
Watching reruns and TV lights.

I'd regret going indoors just to sleep
When the northern lights did dance
Not standing there to watch them
When I'd had that perfect chance.

I'd miss the blazing autumns
With their flaming colors glowing
When mundane chores held me captive
And robbed me of their showing.

I'd wish I'd sat there on that deck
On mornings warm and bright
Hearing finches chirp "Good Morning"
As for each seed they'd fight.

I'd regret not visiting my good friends
Who were lonely, ill that day,
To give them each a little lift
And to cheer them on their way.

So I know not how much time I have
But I know I will be glad
To live each day as if 'twere my last
So my last will not be sad!

Reaching Too High

Sometimes we need to be realistic
Sometimes we need to see
That what we view in Dreamland
Is not what we can be.

Aspirations are all fine and good
If our goals are within reach
But when they go beyond that
They're but lessons meant to teach.

When goals keep getting difficult
And stall us in every action
It's wiser to just turn around
And change our whole direction.

Mount Everest may be the pinnacle
To which we would aspire
But Manitoba's Baldy Mountain
Is our limit! We can't go higher!

'Tis better to just face this world
And function within our limit
Accept the time within our grasp
And live the life that's in it!

Philosophy for Life

Sometimes we hit a snowbank
Sometimes we even get stuck
Sometimes we need a shovel
To change our rotten luck.
It gets so hard to smile again
To overcome distress
We may need to change courses
To get out of the mess.
So when a thing looks hopeless
When we think we've reached the end
Let's get the problem out there
Where we can make it mend.
We need a reassessment
To change our whole perception
All problems look less daunting
On clear and close inspection.
Just purging and exposing
And much investigation
Can be a great catharsis
And cease the castigation.
The problem may just shrink in size
When we see its true proportion
It never really was that bad
And our angst demands abortion.

So smiling at our problems
Is a really good solution
It just takes some time to find
A different resolution!

A Grand Adventure

As I gaze across a memory
Of idealistic youthful dreams
Those hopes and aspirations
That seemed just lacking schemes.

Life's easy from a childish view
From the ignorance of bliss
Accomplishments and visions
Of success seem hard to miss.

But days of youth slip by so fast
And life takes a different course
And suddenly the time has passed
Like a torrent of great force.

We have to change perception
And adjust to meet the strife
Directions change with circumstance
And conditions shape a life.

Some goals that I had chosen
Were not easy to attain
The dreams I thought were simple once
I cannot dream again.

But life has not been futile
It's been shaped by every venture
It's been a rewarding journey
An altered grand adventure!

Once Upon A Future Past

Once upon a future past
I wished for treasures unsurpassed
I wanted things that I could hold
To complete my life, see it unfold

What I couldn't have, I wanted more
To go without was an awful chore
I lived a life of wishful thinking
And dreamed sad dreams, my spirit sinking.

I stopped and looked at life's short span
Which wasted away without a plan
I was being held captive in a timeless grip
I saw life passing, I felt it slip.

Contentment was so hard to find
I must approach it with a different mind
So many things were out of bound
I'd have to turn my life around.

I studied the clouds and began to ponder
I gazed at rainbows and saw the wonder
Mountains held beauty, majestic and steep
Still lakes serene, so peaceful and deep.

Suddenly I found my treasures discovered
They never were hidden, they weren't even covered
Why waste precious life, wishing away
When I could be savouring it each passing day!

Such Is Life

I watched a star through my window last night
As it peeked from the shade of a tree
I wanted to see more of its twinkling light
But the dancing leaves hid it from me.

I focused my eyes on that certain spot
Till the whispering breeze allowed me to see
A few fleeting moments of that glimmer of light
Such brief encounters from behind that tree.

I waited and waited for an hour or two
It seemed like a lifetime was passing me by
But all I could catch was an infrequent glimpse
Just a random twinkle and I wanted to cry.

Why don't those leaves just stop all their dancing?
Why don't they let my star shine through?
Move over, come out, show me its brilliance
I long for much more, just flashes won't do.

I finally left my comfortable chair
(All it took was that minor decision)
Moved to a spot where the tree did not block
That star's silver beam, and my vision.

My star was now glowing, all in full view
Minus those shadows, it glistened so bright
If I had but moved when first I had spied it
I'd have basked in its beam the whole night!

How much like real life, this starlight, I thought
All the time that we waste while we wait
Instead of just moving on with our life
We sit and complain about fate.

We need only to move from the rut that we're in
To find happiness that we're yearning to feel
Let go of the past, reach out to the future
It's there for the taking, it's ours and it's real!

The Value Of A Mistake

From some painful mistake somewhere in our past
A memory will plague us and help to attest
Those actions before us, the things that we do
May have consequences we don't want them to.
The cost of education is expensive, you know,
And money is seldom the force of the blow.
Embarrassing moments keep us from repeating
Some major faux pas, though the blush was but fleeting.
Or some terrible blunder that caused an uproar
Will not re-occur 'cause we've tallied the score.
So cherish those moments when you discover an error
They're lessons so precious, they'll haunt you forever.

Stop For A Minute

As you hurry along life's pathway
And you pause not in your stride
Try stopping for a moment
To enjoy the current ride.
Try smiling at a stranger
Or touch a heart that's sad
Lend a hand to a needy friend
And make that friend feel glad.
Whisper a word of encouragement
To someone who's feeling blue
Hum a tune and very soon
You'll have them humming too.
Try listening to the songbirds
Singing sweetly in the trees
Savour each moment now before you
You'll have beautiful memories.

So command a carefree moment
And free it from all stress
Make the road so much more pleasant
On your climb towards success.

Who Said It Was Impossible

Who said it was impossible to feel comfort through deep pain?
Does a star light not through darkness?
Or the sun not shine through the rain?

Who said it was impossible to find smiles amid the tears?
We all have known some gladness
Over long unhappy years.

Who said it was impossible to find peace where none exists
To reach for truth, to find the root
Where harmony persists.

Who said it was impossible to stand up for the right?
To hold firm against a throng so strong
That you must fall or fight.

Who said it was impossible to reach the rainbow's end?
Amid foes and woes and desperate lows
To find that one true friend

Who said it was impossible from a vortex of distress
To find joy and peace and happiness
At the pinnacle of success.

Who said it was impossible to change a life gone wrong
To right a deed, reshow a seed
And watch it grow up strong.

So collect all those memories of each joy and pain you bore
Make them just your stepping stones
To peace, and love, and more!

Bosses' Day

Hark all you folks that labour
At a job you attend each day
It's time that you gave credit
To the boss who helps you pay
Those mortgages and car loans
And utilities and such
For if you had no job today
You would have to suffer much.
If you can't take them out to lunch
Or spread a banquet grand
Then maybe you could each at least
Give them a grateful hand.
For it's not so easy to be "Boss"
To always be so strong
There're times when they would rather yield
When everything goes wrong.
When unions and the government
Set challenges obscure
Yet still they persevere and stay
To keep those jobs secure.
So all you folks now pause awhile
Stand up and applaud your Boss
For if they were not at the helm
You would surely feel the loss!

Success

I never wished for riches
I never wished for gold
I never dreamed of mansions
To have when I grow old

My dreams were rather simple
Though you may find them quaint
I've never been the "bad one"
But I never was a saint.

Success just meant achieving
A measure of recognition
A line to say I've been here
My goals have reached fruition.

So take your wealth and riches
And enjoy them as you will
I'll enjoy my small successes
That's where I get MY thrill!

A Lifespan

As I gaze across a lifespan
Of life's ever-changing dreams
The twists and turns our lives have crossed
Over many stormy years.
Mountains steep and valleys deep
Wild torrents of surging streams
We conquered all adversities
The highs, lows and in-betweens.

I marvel at the courage
And the fortitude it took
To withstand those raging rapids
Of what should have been a brook.
For life is never just a picnic
As anyone can attest
But only by being positive
Can we put the past to rest.
We weren't promised a rose garden
Or a life of easy picking
We strive, we squirm, we struggle
Our strife is of our making.

Fulfilment Of A Dream

I used to dream a wistful dream
Fulfilment I would find
In a vague goal not yet complete
A secret longing not yet defined.

A haunting dream, persistent
Of a hope that once was baited
By authors, poets, sonnets, odes
A thirst as yet unsated.

The simplest hint of glory
Success of late achieved
A victory in minute doses
My yearning soul relieved.

I'm grateful for the blessing
The fulfillment of this dream
It may not be a monument
But it's a real sunbeam!

A Backward Glance

Musing, remembering, reminiscing
A reverie replete with aspiration and idealistic ambition,
Searching for the right words to convey
Those emotions so embedded in the psyche.
That prophecy spawned of a buoyant confidence
Emboldened by youthful optimism and vague design
Now abounding with achievement incomplete.
An experience untouched by life, as yet unaware.

But there is something disconcerting
Fraught with angst and unease
About exposing –
Or imploding a profile of a life.
Displaying its illusion,
Its passion still pending validation
Its goal still awaiting confirmation
Its tenure still seeking termination
And in so doing
For all life's trials – a recompense!

I'd Like To Be

I'd like to be a blue bird
Trilling lilting melodies
In wild abandon, never ending
Mother Nature's rhapsodies.

I'd like to be a bumblebee
Soaring roaring through the air
Landing softly on the blossoms
Bright and fragrant waiting there.

I'd like to be a perfume
Wafting softly in the breeze
Melding visions, nature's beauty
With wonderful memories.

I'd like to be a dew drop
Shining bright in the morning sun
Sitting on a velvet petal
Of a blossom newly sprung.

I'd like to be a rainbow
Arched above the world so high
Glorious colours softly blending
Like a halo in the sky.

Tranquility

The ultimate serenity
A quiet evening stroll
Where the heart finds its haven
On a quiet country knoll.

In my dreams I often wander
Where time and life stand still
Pausing 'neath the tree top
Where sings the whippoorwill.

Through the quiet of the evening
Through the stillness of the night
Fanning feathers softly utter
The sound of the owl in flight

A hovering pair of nighthawks
Their silent wings unfurled
Gliding slowly o'er this portrait
Of an enchanted wonder world.

The aura of the meadow
Of fresh daisies does proclaim
A wild fragrance none can capture
A sweet perfume none can tame.

With the sigh of an evening zephyr
The angels softly speak
Touching softly as they linger
Like silk upon my cheek.

In the breeze, the trees are swaying
With their branches gently bent
Mother Nature rocking calmly
In her armchair, so content.

In peaceful quiet rapture
My soul perceives its heaven
This Paradise, this Eden
God has so freely given!

<u>Thank You Lord</u>

For good health and life serene

For friends and family often seen

For sunny days and moonlit nights

For heavens full of starry lights

For trees and flowers, around and near

For air we breathe that's sweet and clear

For food enjoyed that sustains our life

For peaceful times that hold no strife

For laughter, joy – and sorrow, too

All life's experiences you guide us through

For all the blessing you give each day

We are truly grateful and we humble pray:

Thank You Lord!

On Thanksgiving Day

As I look back over many years
Days full of joy and full of tears
Big expectations and morbid fears
We faced it all – and made life good.

We laughed, we cried, we danced, we hobbled
Our grim determination merely doubled
Steadfastly denying that we were troubled
By trials that life dumped in our path.

But life was good and life was giving
And through it all we made a living
God was patient – all forgiving
For our ingratitude and complaints.

Now comes the time to recognize
That blessings come in a disguise
With family woes and family ties
That we oft'times fail to appreciate.

For gifts received and gifts rejected
Those gifts we should have all respected
And for the things we least expected
And failed to see their value mount.

So let's bow our heads and give our thanks
For all the people in our ranks
Fond memories in our "data banks"
And a life that's full of blessings still!

Europe's Silent Legacy

Carefree tourists, singing gaily
Age old melodies, simple words
The unfolding panorama of ageless Europe – France
Rushing past our tour bus
As we speed along the highway.

Wide open fields of grain
Thick, lush, seemingly endless
An emerald sea, undulating
Heaving, breathing, sighing
With each gust of the shifting breeze.

Suddenly, the singing voices hush
A gasp! An exclamation!
All eyes turn.
In the midst of the silent growing grain
A massive graveyard!
Countless rows of white crosses
Command our attention.
In stark contrast to the harmony we felt
Just minutes ago.
An eerie chill clambers up our spine
And grim reality battles disbelief.

In the field, the crosses stand
A silent memorial
To brave young men
Strangers in a foreign land
Who fought that war so long ago.
Only silent graveyards remain
Desolate, lonely, unadorned
Amidst a sea of emerald grain.
Just a simple melancholy reminder
Of countless lives laid low
Outsiders in a land not their own
Who gave their lives
That a stranger might live
Might sing. Might laugh.
Might plant these fields of grain
That wave so freely in the wind.

Remembrance Day

With a haunting and poignant pathos
We recall those heroes
We never really knew.
Those unfamiliar faces
Warriors all, bold, intrepid,
Guardians of our freedom borne.

With distant visions yet undefined
Noble passions, valiant aspirations
And willing hearts they faced the dark unknown
They left behind peaceful homes
To wander in uncharted regions
To face distress, life fraught with danger
To bravely fight a war that was not their own.

Can we even ever change age-old ideologies
So unlike our own, yet so ingrained
That foreign concepts just cannot grasp
Nor accept? Nor consider? Nor renounce?
Yet our heroes go to battle
They strive, they struggle, they sacrifice
To make life just a little better
For strangers they will never know!

St. Patrick's Day

I am not a green leprechaun
I'm not Irish through my birth
But I once kissed the Blarney Stone
And I saw St. Paddy's berth.
So from his lofty perch I say
To folks both far and near
I wish you all God's blessings
Throughout the coming year.
I wish for all a future
Of a blissful youthful life
A world of second chances
To fix your trials and strife.
A world that's free of sorrow
A world of happy smiles
A world of pleasing byways
For miles and miles and miles.
A world of such perfection
No evil can conceive
No malice or iniquity
May your peaceful world perceive
I wish you all earth's treasures
And happiness galore
And nowhere be there sadness
It is banished forevermore

Happy St. Paddy's Day to all.

What is Freedom?

Freedom is a priceless endowment Canadians take for granted
Without rancour or apology – or gratitude
It's "our right," our inheritance – our very own
No one may trample it, question it, or disown it
Take it away, disclaim it – or even earn it.
It is there, it is ours – free for the taking
Even if we fail to recognize or appreciate it
Even when we challenge, dispute, distort, or abuse it
It remains with us still.
Unworthy, ungrateful, though we may be
The ever-loving puppy at our feet
Forever faithful, always patient, all forgiving, never judging
Though we be prone to such disdain.

In Canada, freedom is not an elusive, impossible dream
It is not a sad lament, not even a fantasy
Uttered with apprehension or dread
Lest we be overheard.

Our Freedom is not a nebulous vision on a misty horizon
A vague and hopeless delusion, unfruitful, barren
A beautiful mirage of an unattainable aspiration
A wistful thought, unrealized, in fear unspoken
A child not ever-yet to be conceived.

What have I done to be so privileged to possess it?
Worthy and deserving of this incalculable liberty?
I was born in Canada!
As for the suffering million poor of this world –
there, but for the grace of God, go I!!!

Swamp Lights

Swamp lights floating
In the air and over the ground
Small, big, oblong, round
Stopping not for trees or folks
They silently engulf, surround,
Then slowly drift on by.

Illuminating balls of light
Roaming aimlessly through the night
Unattached, unexplained
Just there, in the air, like a flare
Suspended by invisible thread
Hanging from the dark night.
No beginning, no end
Just random balls of light
Floating in the night.

Eclipse Of The Sun

Crescent shadows dancing on the floor
Through the maples 'round my door
Cast from a disk of a crescent sun
Rays of light, demarcated view
Bits of sunlight filtering through
The maple trees with teeming leaves
Dancing in the breeze.

Above
Where the sun was sovereign king
Just a short time ago
Single, alone, in the great beyond
Unchallenged, undisputed, unrivalled.

Now the moon has invaded
The sun's imperial domain
Blocking its regal rays
Impeding its heavenly reign
Obstructing its path of light
Declaring again
Its singular subjugation
But temporary!

Atlantic Storm

I sit quietly on the padded chaise on the "Oceanos" deck
Surrounded by the luxury of an opulent ocean cruise.
From behind the heavy glass walls
I watch the massive waves of the mighty Atlantic Ocean
As they hurl themselves into oblivion
Against the big cruise ship.
Their colossal power, resounding, reverberating
Proclaiming their supremacy with a thunderous roar
As they toss our ship about
Making it cringe and creak under their unrelenting assault.

Yet I feet smug somehow watching their fury
Secure and safe behind that thick glass
"You can't touch me," I taunt
I gloat in my sanctuary.
I watch in awe and exhilaration,
Calm delight and fascination
And experience a unique delight
As I watch those giant whitecaps
Roll menacingly towards us
And tuck us lovingly under their arm with their curl!

Blues

<u>Vanished Dreams</u>

My ship of dreams has left the port
It has sailed out to sea
It crashed into an iceberg
Leaving no real hope for me.

I planned so much for that sortie
I'd outlined the whole deal
But fate stepped in to thwart my plan
My vision for to steal.

It hurts to see my wistful dreams
It wounds my soul so deep
To see them all lie shattered
In a useless crumpled heap.

I lost the goal to work toward
The star that shone so bright
I drift without a paddle now
Through the darkness of the night.

But somewhere there is victory
Somewhere there has to be
A bright new star to light my way
A guidepost just for me.

I'll not succumb to misery
I must fight it all the way
I'll conquer this dejection
I'll sing again someday!

Silent Images

Melancholy glimpses of happy moments
Haunting flashbacks of bygone days
Piercing thoughts in silence screaming
At a mirage of a once beautiful dream
Deformed, mutilated, disfigured,
Distorted by time
Hardened by circumstances
Tarnished by stark reality,
A fading fragrance of hope undaunted
Retreating into a permanent abyss.
In its wake, a poignant heart
Echoing a sorrowful lament
For a life that never was to be!

Whispered Secrets

The wind hisses through the trees
Touching me with a slow seductive caress
Teasing me with a whisper
Taunting my aloneness
Tantalizing my senses
And tempting me with fantasies
Of glowing passions and warm embraces
Intriguing visions beyond the here and now.

It whispers secrets I do not wish to know
Tells me tales I do not want to hear
A flagrant boasting of veiled knowledge
Furtive gossip and stealthy innuendo
That flaunts my indiscretions
As though guilty of the deed.

I sit there cringing
Accountable for — I know not what
I tune the hiss out
And the whisper
Yet it assuages my conscience not.

The sun glares at me from above
The Eye of Judgement
Condemning me
For this game I did not wish to play.

Searching

Searching for peace
In a sea of turmoil
My heart a knot, I cannot untie
Where do I go to escape this plunder?
Of vanishing visions of lifelong dreams
This endless longing
That plagues my life
And tears my every thought apart.
I look ahead as through a window
Into an ever darkening night
A black abyss is all around me
Is there serenity within my sight?
My quest for happiness, long enduring
Sighs from deep within my soul
Seeking something so elusive
Can I name it?
I fear not!
Relax my soul
Still your yearning
Accept the crumbs that you are dealt
Accept, for there is no tomorrow
No radiant glow to light your path!
Accept! Agree! Allow! Submit!

__Condemned__

Condemned for something I haven't done
By someone that I thought I knew
For something, they only think is me
Condemned, because they cannot see
The things that only God can see.

If they only knew the real me
If the actual truth they could but see
The truth that must so hidden be.

Like vultures watching an ailing calf
They wait to rush in for the kill
The truth they do not wish to seek
Lest they should find there,
Conscious fabrication.

'Tis better to just judge, condemn
Than challenge credence openly
Prolong the falsehood, defy, maintain
Than feel compelled words to recall.
A truth which invisible must remain.

But God above can see it all
He knows the wrongs of everyone
And someday when that judgement falls
HIS justice! It shall come to be!

Gloom!

In the shadows of despair
Anguish is my intimate friend,
My constant companion
The silent shadow at my heels
Cheer – 'tis but a lie – repeated.....
The false façade for my secret pain
The negative force for my positive stride.

Like a fog, the uncertainty – thick, relentless
A tide of pessimism I cannot control
Gripping, crippling,
Suffocating my ailing confidence.

In vain I grope for truth and justice
I search for solace, fruitlessly
Some crumb of faith to stave my yearning
A soothing balm for my aching soul.

Like a drowning waif in a pool of quicksand
I thrash against assaulting fear
I fight despair, shun depression,
Repress anxiety with no success.
I sense betrayal, strong and forceful
(There's little hope of a mistake)
No calm awareness of peace evolving
To stem the tide of overwhelming grief.

Caverns Of My Mind

Within the caverns of my mind
Stark black chasms, grotesque and grey
Stretch like tunnels to infinity.
In gaping grottos, crowded with emotions
Haunting, dispirited memories
Hover like phantoms of an illusion
Glowing, in the darkness of deep thought.

Gloomy impressions of life's upheavals
Fleeting morbid images of the past
Ebony drips of shorn reflections
Like iridescent dewdrops
That never, ever catch the light.

Frosty icicles with jagged edges
The spikes of anguish, sorrow, grief
Like cold stalactites that weep forever
Unto opaque and murky stalagmites
Protruding from a floor of agony.
Sad regrets, unearned reprisals
Stifling, choking my every gasp.

<u>Victory</u>

Trapped by memories of better days
Tied to a past that won't let me go
Barriers, obstacles weigh me down
Why can't they leave me now alone?
Where the justice? Where the truth?
When does life begin anew?
Where the answers? Where the peace?
Where that perfect solitude?

A bitter world I'll not accept,
I'll make this torment flounder
This angry froth of stormy waves,
I will defeat and conquer.
My lonely heart I'll not expose,
No eyes shall see me weep
No ear will hear my mournful cry,
Nor feel my pain so deep.
I'll not succumb, I'll live again,
I'll let the sun shine through
I'll fight despair, I'll fix my smile,
I'll win this battle too.

When over those darkened hours I've trod
My anguish all beneath me
My weary soul will triumph find
In pained heartache – a victory!

Triumph At Last

Should I go ere morning breaks
I shall go undaunted
My insecurities now receding
My foremost fears are thwarted
Through a window shines the sun
Its beams now cast a glow
Seeds of contentment now are sprouting
Dare I trust that they will grow?
There's a different age evolving
I can see this to be truth
There's glimmer of optimism growing
The hope of harmony glowing
The budding blooms of serenity showing
That desperate desolation slowly going
Oh that I might live again!

From My Heart

<u>Goodbye LouLou My Friend</u>

You tiptoed into my life so softly,
A loving heart, a feeble breath
A pleasant word, a genuine smile
An eager welcome, forthcoming chat.

You asked for nothing, demanded little.
Just above a whisper, you only begged
"No, don't go yet, stay a bit longer"
Your frail delicate voice entreated
And I could not leave you so forlorn.

I hardly felt you pierce my heart
You entered so discreetly
Just a pleasant afternoon escape
But you curled into my soul so deeply
And made my heart your "home sweet home."

Your resilient spirit is my beacon
Your enormous foot prints my guiding path
I'll nev'r forget those fond portrayals
Of the highs and lows that shaped your life.
So sleep my friend, sweet thy slumber
Away from weary pain, distress,
Sleep, for someday I will join you
And we'll continue from where we left off.

Sweet Surrender

She sits in her padded armchair
Swaying gently back and forth
Frail, fragile, and pathetic
As soft moans haunt each breath
She pleads not to be left alone.
Alone in a bleak world.
Alone with her memories.

"No, don't leave yet," she implores me
Her feeble voice quivers, weak,
A poignant mixture of sadness, hope
Forlorn, forgotten, forsaken.
Her eyes are pools of aged longing
And her plaintive pleading spears my heart.

"But you look tired, you need to rest, Dear."
I search to find the gentle words
To dispel rejection, disown indifference
And I make a promise I aim to keep
"I'll come back later, when you have rested.
It won't be long, so rest my dear."

Slowly, painfully, but with resolve,
She moves her head from side to side
"Oh I'm just fine, I'll rest later."
She strains to raise her sagging form.
A valiant effort of ageless endurance
Against the onslaught of weighted years.
Declining health has sapped her vigor
But age has failed to quell a spirit
That just won't falter or be stilled.

So I sit back down and we reminisce
Of carefree days so long now gone.

Forever Lost

He stands alone, weeping, broken
Pathetic, shattered and forlorn.
Words surround him, he can hear them
Curses, obscenities, vile, irate.
Words he never thought she'd known.

Seated before him – an angry woman
Not the mother he used to know
That loving nature, forever giving
That generous soul with ne'er a foe
Decorous persona, serene and tender
With a heart so pure it defied all scorn!

But somewhere from the depths of evil
A cruel disease had o'rpowered her brain
Had turned that sweetness into rancour
And acrimony, unprovoked, unbidden
Had claimed authority o'er her reign.

Now broken-hearted, her son stands sobbing
Before a mother who remembers not
Those years now gone, so full of promise
Of sweet devotion and compassion,
A life of glorious family love.
A doting mother she had once been
Cooing love songs to her spawn
Cradling children to her bosom
In her ever-loving arms
That mother love's now but a memory
A mother whose son now mourns as gone!

Yesteryears

Amid thoughts that wander, stray and ramble
And memories all so poignant still
She sits alone rocking gently.
With sinking heart, tear-filled eyes.
On feeble legs she strolls through time.

She dreams, envisions and revisits
Those yesteryears so long since gone.
A distant past now, not forgotten
A life with pleasures and delights
A life with sunshine and with shadows
When life was full and graced with love.

Those days are gone but she remembers
Those intense moments of lows and highs
A steady stream of tears and laughter
Youthful spirit, exuberance, joy
A life now but a memory.

And she sits and rocks – alone.

My Lonely World

You came into my world today
You saw, you understood
The presence of a poignant loss
Of something sweet and good
You gazed into my woeful eyes
Your sympathy profound
My smile was weak, my outlook bleak
Your empathy was sound.
You held my shaking hand awhile
My fingers you caressed
My face was blank but in my mind
I knew you were distressed.

My dynamic life has faded now
Its exuberance diminished
My vibrant verve nonexistent now
My zest for life is finished
I appreciate your kindness
I am grateful for your caring
But compassion now is bittersweet
As the Pity you are sharing.
We cannot turn back the hands of time
Or control our aging progression
We but hope to face with a calming grace
The end – without depression.

Small Beginnings

I recall my father singing,
As he carded wool each night
And my mother sat there spinning
Near a coal oil lamp's dim light.

My brother and I knitted
Socks and mittens by the score
Each new pair that was completed
To be added to our "store."

But the "store" was always empty
As our neighbours checked supplies
And as quickly as we made them
They were there for instant buys.

This precious family business
Though meagre, we'll agree
Was what gave us pride and pleasure
Self-respect and dignity.

A Life That Was Never Meant To Be

Sadly she gazes at a photo
In black and white, taken long ago
A baby girl, so sweet and precious
A life to cherish and watch her grow.

She sees a life of bliss, contentment
Her little family is growing fast
Her hopes, her dreams, her life evolving
Her fervent prayer comes true at last.

She pictures images of great successes
She smiles with pleasure and delight
At stumbling steps, and proms, and grad nights
Those wondrous "firsts" for her neophyte,

Her maternal heart dreams, envisions
Such timeless pleasures, with wistful thrill
A golden future of life's great moments
A glorious prophesy yet to fulfill.

She sees a wedding, a bride so radiant
A white mirage floating down the aisle
An apparition of life enraptured
Her heart so full it lights her smile.

But fate was cruel and life was stolen
Those dreams she'll never come to see
A poignant memory still full of sorrow
That perfect life never meant to be.

Rambling Memories Of Kulish

As I rush about my duties
Of my very busy day
I recall those blissful moments
When I'd had the time to play.

Those blissful carefree moments
On those days so long ago
In that wonderful place called Kulish
Where wild berries used to grow.

There is little now left standing
Of those golden times of old
The old schoolhouse now holds bushels
Of grain grown but yet unsold.

Miles of open grain fields
Wave where trees and forest stood
Where the songbirds trilled their pleasure
And proclaimed that life was good.

The homes that we once lived in
Have been bulldozed down like trees
But we'll see them all in heaven
In a blaze of memories.

We never rode the school bus
But we walked the route with love
Down the road that was a tunnel
With tall trees that met above.

All those Christmas decorations
Those school concerts we put on
And then walking home at midnight
Two long miles of snow and fun.

I recall the joyous Easters
By the Church we'd have our Plays
That big bell did not stop ringing
For three glorious happy days.

That beloved church from Kulish
Where we solemnly came to pray
Where God reached down to bless us
Is now just ashes far away.

My heart still melts a little
And my eyes with tears still fill
At the touch of a western zephyr
Or the song of a whippoorwill.

When I grow too old and feeble
When I can rush no more
I'll just remember Kulish
And my heart again will soar.

We Can't Go Back

We can't go back
To youthful carefree days
When life stood still
And heaven was just a touch away.
When a simple evening walk
Brought wonder, ecstasy, – and love
A shared happiness so complete
It transcended simple words.

You walked me home that night
And your touch sent my senses reeling
As your shoulder brushed mine
With a faltered step
On an unexpected rock in the shadows below.

For one brief moment, you held me tight
And entrapped my heart.

You kissed me then
Oh, so shyly – yet ever so tenderly
On my cheek.

I was too shy to kiss you back
To put my arms around you
But I yearned for that moment to last
Last forever,
Wrapped tightly in your embrace.

When you left,
You took a piece of my heart with you
And I didn't wash my face for a week
Lest I wash off
That precious, sweet and tender kiss
You had bestowed upon my cheek.

Our lives changed when we moved away
Silently and in secret, I kept dreaming
But our paths never crossed again.

My broken heart healed
And life went on.
We became different people
With different lives
Different goals
Different loves...

But the memory of that first love remained
Buried deep within my heart
To surface in those secret moments
When I walk alone in the dark
Stumble on a rock
And falter in my step....

A single shy peck upon my cheek
Still sears my face
As though a flame....
And the wonder of that first love
Still warms my aging heart.

Grandma's Pride And Joy

Cheeks like petals, rosy, glowing
Beguiling smile that melts the heart
Eyes like twinkling stars, so knowing
Enticing, charming, dazzling, dark.

Silken arms entwined securely
Round my neck so tightly wrapped
Simple love, proclaimed demurely
Holds my captured heart entrapped.

Enchanting curls, like ribbons dancing
With each toss of the golden hair
Precocious laughter, love enhancing
Chimes like music through the air.

All life's worries fade and fracture
Like those dewdrops in the sun
Heart that swells in blissful rapture
Peaceful love from Heaven spun.

Little angel, nodding, sleeping
Now resting peaceful as a dove
In my arms my vigil keeping
O'er Grandma's pride, and joy, and love!

Daisy Was A Lady – Once

Daisy was a lady
Once
With poise and grace
And elegance and pride.
Her eyes were bright, her speech refined,
There was purpose in her stride.
Folks sought her counsel
For her words were wise
And her ideals were honourable.
All who knew her
Were proud to call her "Friend."
They listened as she spoke
Their attention undivided,
For Daisy was a lady
Then.

We see her now
Just the shell
Of the Daisy we used to know.
Age has taken its toll,
But it's the dreaded disease
That has ravaged her soul
And stripped her of that dignity
She worked so hard to maintain;
The respect that was hers alone;
That took a lifetime to build.
That flawless reputation
Carved by perseverance and determination,
Is all but a memory now,
In the minds of those who know
That Daisy was a lady
Once

We barely recognize her face
So sullen, disinterested
Devoid of the bright smile of recognition;
Her eyes staring blankly into space
Avoiding contact with humanity
As if we were some alien race
To whom she has nothing to say.

She is oh, so different now
Her shoulders stoop
Her head hangs low
And her steps falter
As she shuffles aimlessly through the halls
Of the nursing home where she now resides.
Visitors pass her by
With pity in their eyes
For she remembers not
The people she held so dear
When Daisy was a lady.

She had a husband once
A loving family
Whose very existence was intertwined with hers.
They laughed together in the good times
Cried together when things were bad;
They worked and played
And prayed together for the same goals.
Their aspirations rose and fell as one.

Now their visits seem so meaningless,
For Daisy does not know they're there.
She knows not who they are,
Just another voice,
Another face in an endless abyss,
Another form in her wandering path,
A form from the distant past,
When Daisy was a lady.

Her children come
Now with families of their own
Their hearts bleed
And their eyes fill with unshed tears
To see this pathetic figure
Who's not the mother they once knew,
When Daisy was a lady.

But there is a part
They still recognize.
Daisy carries a doll now
She holds her close
Enfolding her to her bosom
Gazing at the doll with a love so profound
That time itself retracts its sequence
The children watch
And remember.......
When Daisy was a lady.

Faraway Roots

A city far away
Strange and unfamiliar
In a restaurant, simple, homey
I sit staring, unbelieving
At a placement – unique, yet unpretentious
"Just a bit of nostalgia" they called it
"True Canadiana" they said
Just random photos of bygone days
Reproduced and printed
On white parchment with scalloped edges
Decorated with an antique scrolled design.

But the picture on that parchment is not insignificant
The people in that snapshot are not nameless!
Where did it come from?
How did it get here?
This picture of my old home
The house with the whitewashed walls
And the double window that faced the morning sun.
My brother and I
Standing just knee high
To our older grown up sisters, brother
Solemnly posing on the front steps
Those steps that my father built
From wood that stood behind the old shed.
And mother coming towards us
Along the picketed flower bed
With a sidewise glance at the photographer.

I gaze in awe at my past
Looking back at me through years of time
And wonder at this marvel
Prompted by a stranger unaware.

Not insignificant, this picture
It's me, my roots, my childhood home!
My early youth,
So long forgotten
By a stranger unknowingly resurrected.

A house no one considered important
A family no one recognized but me
This home looking back at me
From this picture in a stranger's unlikely abode
In this faraway place of "now."

Friend

What do I see when I look at you
I see the bright sun shining through
A cloudless sky of azure blue
A lovely rose that's sprung anew.
I see a friend that's always true
I see pure love reflected too,
And I see you smile like you always do.
So what do I feel when I think of you
I feel so grateful, I know you!

You Are My Soulmate

Little did I know those years ago
Just where we'd be today
I really didn't believe the words
You kept telling me each day.

I knew I'd found a soulmate
When you slipped into my world
You stayed around and listened
And my love for life unfurled

You looked at me so simply
With those imploring puppy eyes
I never could resist them
Or those ever wistful sighs.

I tried hard to be sensible
To do what I thought I should
But I couldn't turn my back on you
E'en when I wished I could.

And now you've changed my life around
And turned it inside out
No matter what the people say
I now cannot back out!

'Cause I have fallen far too deep
In love with you my friend
And I know whatever life will bring
I'll love you to the end!

Birthday Gifts

A cup to keep your dreams in
To sip from every day.
To keep you warm and glowing
And to lead you where they may.

A bag to collect your wishes
And make them all come true
With a prayer for God's assistance
'Cause He's always there for you.

A halo to keep you kind and good
A song to make you smile
Some promising new challenges
To make your life worthwhile.

Warm, balmy summer evenings
To put stars into your eyes
Good fortune at your footsteps
As signs of God's replies.

Birthdays Past

Your birthday's a time to remember
The years that have gone before
The coloring book
The rides on "Duke"
And wall to wall kids on the floor.

The picnics we had with the "clam bake"
The dunking you took at Singoosh Lake
Quiet little Sandy Beach
The week-long "Swimmer's Itch"
And those gosh awful spiders, for Goodness sake.

Often my good advice you spurned
From each mistake you always learned
I watched in admiration
With no slight fascination
As you realized each success that you'd earned!

So your birthday is a time to look forward
To the years that are yet to be
But I want you to know
That wherever you go
You'll always be "my little girl" to me!

Keep Your Happiness Glowing

There's a warm and bright sun shining
Though clouds may be dark outside.
When your happiness beams across your face
And your smile spreads to your eyes.

I need to know you're happy
That there's no sorrow in your life
That peace reigns in your heart each day
That you never suffer strife.

So keep the sunshine glowing
In your life and in your heart
For even if our paths divide
In my life you'll share a part.

A Seventeenth Birthday

So you're seventeen and the world is new
And all around you there're things to do
Places to go, people to see
A life to explore, a mission to decree.
But you'll do well, my child so dear
'Cause you're a "good kid" from what I hear.
You're full of life, and love, and joy
And life for you is a learning toy.
You take the knocks and learn their lesson
And apply it to your life with passion.
So go with gusto, march with pride
For you've a fire that you can't hide
That love for life will see you through
And I really am so proud of you.
You'll make your mark on history's pages
I know you'll be there with the sages
My love for you is great, it's true
As is my faith that you'll come through
You'll make us glad, you'll make us proud
You'll make us sing your song out loud.
So have a happy birthday, dear,
You'll conquer this old world, don't fear!

A Special Love

There's special warmth within my heart
It explodes with every meeting
When I can see that certain smile
And my love calls out a greeting.

The sun is always shining
Though the rain may try to fall
For when I hold his hand in mine,
Our love can conquer all!

I never thought I'd feel it
Such tender warm emotion
It pulses through my every vein
Like a strong and mighty potion.

I thank the Lord above me
In silent fervent prayer
For giving me this chance to know
Such special love is there!

Sunshine Of My Life

I thought my life was over
There was no more love to go
Then I found your arms around me
And I felt the sunshine glow.
My heart once more was pounding
A heaven on earth began
How is it that a life can change
With the love of a special man?
I wake each morning daily
Facing life with a happy smile
For I know that when I see you
You'll make my day worthwhile.
I love you oh so dearly
My life is now my symphony.
I thank the Lord above me
For sending you to me!

Missing My Poetry

My poetic tire was hissing
There was no more air inside
I knew something was missing
I thought my brain was fried

My wheels were turning slower
There was no more oomph or speed
I must man that pump with power
Or hire myself a steed.

My zest for verse is getting rough
I can feel it shutting down
If I don't get off my old fat duff
My faculties will drown.

I've gone to prose and story
That's not a problem yet
But verse in all its glory
Is a thrill I can't forget.

So bear with me in patience
While I get air to those tires
I will regain my licence
Before my term expires!

Losing Ground

When your tricky brain goes AWOL
And you feel you're losing ground
And the thought you're trying to retrieve
Just doesn't hang around.
You try hard to remember
But it seems to no avail
You may as well be hauling rain
In a leaky water pail.
Your mind gets so frustrated
And you fear the end is near
You seem so close to losing all
The brainpower you held dear.
You fight the sinking feeling
You're aging much too fast
You're so afraid that intellect
Your clever self has passed
Your wit that used to be so sharp
Has hardly now an edge
To get a thought delivered now
You almost need a dredge
Your youthful vim and vigour
Is gone without a trace
It did not stay to bid adieu
Just left you in disgrace
It's sad to know you're failing
And worse to be aware
That all that worldly wisdom
Is just not yours to share.

Mid-Thought Rests

When patience fails, gets mushy
And logic takes a powder
Waning wits, tangled thoughts
Announce our flaws much louder.
It's not that we don't mean well
It's not that we don't care
It's just that we now operate
On a totally different fare
It's not that we are senile
'Cause we know just what is wrong
We'll get it out eventually
It's just waiting on our tongue
It just takes a little longer
For our words to reach your ears
We've just used up our slick tricks
Over all those many years

You bright and nimble young things
Don't laugh or ridicule
You think that you'll outsmart it
And change the aging rule
But that's not how the rules work
As us old folks can attest
We're just slower than we used to be
'Cause we're taking a mid-thought rest!

Now I Am A Snowman

I am not crying the blues
I've no reason to complain
Winter's here, my nose is cold
But I can take the pain.

'Twas really not a bad way
To start a new day free
Till I ran into a snow blower
A blizzard just for me

I tried to duck but to no avail.
To hide, get outta the way
But he was on a mission
He had the right-of-way

Refusing to heed my plight
He just kept on blowing snow
I almost got buried alive
But 'twasn't my time to go.

So now I am a snowman
With nose and eyes with tears
I'm waiting for the sunshine
To come and thaw my ears.

<u>Are We There Yet</u>

As our years keep marching on
And we look back at our past
In childlike wonder we question fate
Are we there yet?
Did we fulfill our destiny already?
How much farther can we go?
Do we dare to still aspire
Can we actually go higher?
Do we dare to try for more?
Could we reach for goals, hope to own
Some vague triumph as yet unknown?

As you ponder at the wonder
Of life's journey and reflect
Do you wonder where you're heading?
How much farther you can get?

We've all come far from where we started
Traversing life's ever winding curves
Blindly, boldly down uncharted byways
Always searching for that illusive dream.
That we just can't forget.

Life's a tour of woes and wishes
Some of them are so far-fetched
But life itself has been a lesson
How life can speed – or change – or cease
And we wonder, "Are we there yet????"

My Scale is Broke

Along with a million others
I decided to lose some weight
To shed those extra inches
Protruding around my waist.

I thought it should be easy
'Cause my numbers were still few
But let me tell you straight, folks
Losing weight is hard to do.

Whether you're fighting with ten or twenty
Or a hundred or two
You're fighting that same old battle
Against commercial crazy glue!

Those pounds are stuck as solid
They're determined to stay on
Shedding them's much harder
Than it was to put them on.

The times I was distracted
By treats of forbidden pleasure
Have added to my poundage
And doubled up my "measure."

By indulging those evil taste buds
By succumbing to temptation
I have to pay the piper now
And suffer through starvation.

No matter how I try to lose
No matter how I pay
The scale refuses to go down
Those pounds are there to stay.

I only sinned "alittle"
But the pounds did multiply
A few pounds turned to twenty
It just makes me wanna cry!

I Heard A Robin Sing

The sun is shining brightly
Its rays are welcome, warm
White clouds are drifting in the sky
With no raindrops falling down
No thunder do I hear today
Though we could use the rain
So I sit and bask in perfect calm
And I hear a robin sing!

The cherry trees are blooming
And the apple, berry, plum,
Their petals keep on floating down
Like confetti tossed around.
It smells like heaven's come to earth
Boundless blessings on the wing
Life so wonderful and grand
'Cause I hear the robin sing!

The roadsides are a blaze of yellow
Amid grasses lush and green
The dandelion is the sovereign here
It's reign is full, supreme
And over and above it all
I hear the robin sing!

The gardener busily mows lawn
In anticipation of some rain
A bunny watches warily
And I hear a robin sing!

The geese are honking overhead
As through the skies they roam
The sparrows gather moss and twigs
To build somewhere a home
(They've given up on nesting in
A birdhouse not meant for them.)
They scold and squawk and make a fuss
They're too big to fit in
I smile at their frustration
And I hear the robin sing!

All spring is in its glory
Nature's bounty and its whim
I've waited for so long it seems
To hear that robin sing

I've planted all those pansies
Their blooms are smiling now
The sun caresses each new face
As in the breeze they bow
God's beauty's all around me
For I hear the robin sing.

I thrill in the perfect solitude
As I sit, survey the scene
My wish came true today it seems
'Cause I heard a robin sing!

A Summer Dream

I've waited with wistful patience
For summer's warmth, and sun, and rain
I've searched the heavens for the showers
But clouds promise rain in vain

If I were out in prairie woodland
Beyond spongy marshland gates
I'd be listening to the frog songs
Croaking love songs to their mates.

But a city confines nature
To these busy numbered streets
It sets limits on our pleasures
And it rations all our treats.

I still recall those spring sounds
That brought pleasures long ago
So I adjust my expectations
To delights that I now know.

It's been a long and dreary winter
And we're due for summer's glee.
I've got most of my wishes granted
My life's a wondrous rhapsody!

Slowspeed

Oh what a hopeless race I run
As I vainly struggle to hang on
My days too short, my hours too few
To complete the tasks that I must do
My goals increase as I stretch my dreams
I divide the time to patch the seams
My mind is flying in all directions
No thought concluded, just multi-fractions
I chase about at hyper speed
And lose all sight of what I need
The things I need, I must confess
To get myself out of this mess
Are simple enough, no fancy frills
No drastic drugs or doctor's pills
An attitude adjustment is where it's at
A turn around to tell me that
The things I dread don't really matter
To forget about them may e'en be better
I need exposure to lighter things
The magic lull when a bluebird sings
That golden moment when day is done
A few more winks of sleep at dawn
The promise of pleasure uncurtailed
A haunting melody my sense assailed
The wafting fragrance of a rose,
All I need is just – repose!

Winter Wonderland

The Celestial Goose has moulted
Shedding down upon the earth
Soft and light, glistening white
Crystal feathers for rebirth.
Heavenly angels guide these feathers
Dusting trees and fields alike
Covering all God's precious treasures
With a duvet, thick and light.
Every tree a thing of beauty
Every park a wonderland
Shining brightly in the sunlight
So adorned by Heaven's hand.
Every pathway, every byway
Deep and white beneath our feet
Beckons searching souls to wander
Where the earth and sky do meet.
No one dares disturb the wonder
Disarrange its beauty deep
For beneath this cosy splendour
All spring's blossoms lie asleep.

Yesterday The Trees Were Bare

Yesterday the trees were bare
Tiny buds of green
Snugly cocooned in miniature maroon blankets
Peered cautiously from minute peepholes
Imprisoned by the chilly gloom around them.
They waited, poised, ready to explode
At the first soft rays of the warm spring sun.
But the clouds continued into the night
No rain, no thunderous roar
Just dull dreary cold
That held everything captive.

Today, the sun
Banished all the clouds away
Conquered, defeated the cold wind
And smiled warmly upon the earth
With a triumphant glow.

The impatient trees burst forth
Unleashing intricately pleated leaves
Emerging from tiny package pods
Dancing for joy
In the soft warm breeze
And all nature beamed its pleasure!

My Roses

I've got my rose bedroom, with accents dark grey
I'm changing my "Image" to spruce up my day
To brighten my world, the way that I feel
This room's the beginning, the source of my zeal

When you see my rose bedroom, you may turn and run
But all I can think of, is I'm having such fun
No more woozy blues now, no sensible greys
I'm aiming for bold now and I'm looking for ways.
To forget all the gloom, to shout from on high.
I'm living for me now and I'm ready to fly.

One wall now has flowers so big and so bright
The charcoal dark background stands out against white
Those big bold gay flowers where none were before
Speak louder than words can and they all underscore
The drabness I have left behind, a new freedom gained
They proclaim oh so loudly of independence attained!
They sing and they laugh through darkness and light
And never, but NEVER! do they darken my night!!!

Selling My Books

People wander on by
Eyeing my display
Afraid to look closer
Lest they be asked to pay.

Relax my friend, don't be afraid
For here's the way I see it
If I must make you buy the book
Then you may never read it.

So stop and look, I won't attack
I will not make you buy
It would not serve my purpose, pal
And here's the reason why.

It's not your chain I want to yank
Your obligation I wish to pin
If your interest I can not peak
Your approval I won't win.

For sales success would bitter be
If you wish you had escaped me
If my sale be but a force-fed pill
Such mockery would plague me.

Your bucks may simply help defray
A costly, mega chore
But only if you like my words
Will you come back for more.

My Computer Lost Its Harddrive

I used to be full of ideas,
For subjects to write about
But something wiped my harddrive
And I have lost my clout.

My personal computer
That ran my brain before
Has been cleaned out of Memory
It won't compute no more.

I sit forlornly at my chair,
My whole body in a hush
I try to jiggle that old brain
But it has turned to mush.

When I lost my old computer
My old harddrive it did die
Now I just feel so empty
'Cause my new harddrive is dry

I have to find some software
And reprogram this old brain
To work with windows Seven
So I can work again

I thought I could escape it
By avoiding Windows Eight
But all this new technology
Has sealed this old brain's fate.

I guess I'll have to just adapt
And join this new rat race
Otherwise I'll keep losing ground
And admit to losing face!

Oh Woe is Me

The Little Lamplight

I'm just a little lamplight
But I'll work with all my might
To pretty up your bedroom
And glow for you at night.

Now I know you won't be reading
Or wanting that extra spark
But just in case you wake up
You won't be in the dark.

So turn me on whenever
You feel the urge to coo
For every time you turn me on
Your wishes will come true.

Walking Bentley (The Dog)

He tugs so eagerly on the leash
As he tows me forward forcefully
He's barely bigger than a rabbit
Yet he's a Clydesdale horse to me.

My dragging gait must be frustrating
He pants and wheezes with all his might
Yet he's relentless as he tows me
His collar's choking him so tight.

I know he loves to run afield
Or down the street with someone young
But this old grandma can't go far past
Five city blocks or what's beyond.

So we struggle hard against each other
He's pulling forth while I pull back
After several blocks of constant pulling
We are both ready for some slack.

This half hour of strenuous exercise
Is most enough to set my day
But Bentley's ready for another
Oh how I'd love to feel that way.

My carefree days are gone forever
As I amble so laboriously
But Bentley smiles in adoration
Just happy to be towing me.

Is It Fall Yet

I walk outside and I see altered
That scene of summer's somehow faltered
The sun behind the clouds keeps hiding
Its orbit's changed, it's lower riding.
It's cooler now I hear the call
I feel the chill of early fall
The rays of heat, the sun's bright glare
It's gone somewhere, it isn't there.
The birds that lilted lovely strands
Have flown away to distant lands.
The flowers bow their heads and sway
They fold their petals as if to pray.
The leaves above in trees still dance
Revel green, it's their last chance
Jack Frost is skulking around the bend
He's marking time for when to send
The vibrant colors of summer's glory
The sign of autumn, the age-old story.
September's here, the time is spent
I don't know where the summer went.
I'm looking forward to the rustle
Of fallen leaves as I rush and bustle.
To clear the garden, the final reaping
Of Nature's bounty for winter keeping
I could go on endlessly,
Reciting blessing ceaselessly,
But 'tis enough to make us treasure
A life so full it's beyond measure!

Holding My Breath

I heard a crow the other day
The geese have honked all day
Seagulls screech all 'round us
But that snow just won't go 'way.

The temperatures scream "Winter"
They refuse to loosen their grip
They force boots onto our cold feet
And warm longjohns on our hip.

We can't forgo our parkas
Or the earmuffs for our ears
Though the sun seems warm from above
That icy wind brings tears.

Somewhere a bird calls "spring-time"
But she really has no inkling
Of the torment she is causing
I don't know what she's thinking

Perhaps I should be patient
But I've been that for so long
It hasn't brought that pleasure
I still pine for the robin's song.

I want to see the green grass
And I know you think I'm lyin'
I'd even welcome all the lowly weeds
And that pesky dandelion!

My Frustrating Computer

My computer is a cantankerous soul
Its aim is to unsettle
To bite me when I least expect
To encounter a stinging nettle.

I try so hard to be consistent
Not to ruffle its fine feathers
But still it seems to take offence
And ignores what I think matters.

It hides my curser, or stops it dead
Then makes me type so small
I never did select that font
That was not my fault at all.

My temper's rising as I type
It makes my blood run cold
It moved this section to the end
And made it all in bold.

It highlights in bright red ink
A somewhat brazen passage
It makes me cringe and hide with shame
That I ever sent that message.

It poings in laughter at my fury
My aggravation, its hilarity
It makes a joke of my persona
And a mockery of my charity.

I am convinced there is a demon
Lurking behind those keystrokes
Its purpose, to torment us
Innocent, unsuspecting, old folks.

Time To Go

The clock ticks on relentlessly
Towards the hour
When I must leave this peaceful haven.
Bid farewell to the tiny yellow flicker
Outside my window
Peering into my trailer
And beguiling me with his song.
Farewell to the pretty butterfly
Sipping nectar from the delicate cherry blossoms
That brush against the window
As they bow to the wind.
Abandon this endless green
That waves and hisses around my trailer
And casts flickering shadows on my table
As the sun sinks ever lower
Heralding the onslaught of day's end.

No! No! No!
Stay up! Stay up!
Give me but a few more hours
To enjoy this bliss
Inhale its serenity
And absorb its peace
So that I may take it with me
A shield of idyllic balm
When I go back to my work-filled world.

Making Peace With My Computer

I've made peace with my computer
As a way of saving face
I don't ask for special favours
It's my only saving grace.
It's been a long time coming
It's very far past due
I don't ask for fancy tricks now
And no snubbing it will do.
I may not like its attitude
But I won't let it irk my ire
I'll keep my calm demeanour
I won't let my temper fire.
So now we've called a final truce
My only chance to win
The cranky thing will not give up
And I won't commit more sin! (*&#%$@)

About The Author

Born in Mossey River, Manitoba, and raised as a farm girl near Ethelbert, Manitoba, Cassie got interested in writing almost as soon as she learned to read. She had little time to pursue that dream until after retirement. Married to an Ethelbert farmer, Cassie took an active role in the farming operations while raising 3 children. Being resourceful, she found pleasure in many creative ways to financial viability.

In 1977, Cassie went back to school to obtain her Grade 12, graduating one year after the last of her children! She took night courses in business and obtained her dream job as a secretary, a position she held for twenty years until retirement in 1999.

From 1980 to 2006, Cassie traveled not only on the continent but also worldwide and kept detailed travel logs of these highlights of her life. Delighting in her retirement, she has turned to writing. She relates her biography in her two published memoirs.

She has also published a novel and a children's book. "*Images of a Pensive Mind*" is her first book of poetry. Currently she's working on another novel and also blogs regularly online at www.cassiesroom.blogspot.ca

Other Books By This Author

Roots ~ A Life In Review *(memoir)*

Sally Snowflake's Christmas *(children's book)*

Small Beginnings *(memoir)*

The Secret In Her Heart *(novel)*

~ ~

For more details on these books, go to:

www.lulu.com/spotlight/cmerko

~ ~